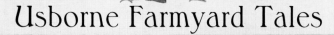

Usborne Farmyard Tales

Christmas Activities

Anna Milbourne

Designed by Non Figg
Illustrated by Stephen Cartwright
and Molly Sage

Photographs by Howard Allman

Contents

There is a little yellow duck for you to find on every double page.

This is Apple Tree Farm.

Mr. and Mrs. Boot live here with their
two children, Poppy and Sam. They
have a dog called Rusty and a cat
called Whiskers. Ted drives the tractor
and helps out on the farm. They are all
busy getting ready for Christmas.

Poppy's sparkly snowflakes

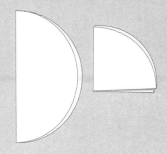

1. Put a mug on top of a piece of white paper. Use a pencil to draw around the mug.

2. Cut out the circle you have drawn. Fold it in half, and then fold it in half again.

3. Using a pair of scissors, cut little shapes out of the paper. Cut a tiny piece off the pointed end, too.

4. Open out the circle. The cut-out pattern makes a snowflake. Glue sequins and glitter onto it.

5. Put the mug on a piece of tissue paper. Draw around it. Then, cut out the circle of tissue paper.

6. Put dots of glue on the back of the snowflake and press the tissue onto it. Tape it in a window.

Sam's carrot-print robins

Wash the spoon between spreading each different paint.

Throw this piece away.

1. Fold three kitchen paper towels and lay them on top of some old newspapers.

2. Pour brown, red and white paint onto the paper towels. Spread the paint with the back of a spoon.

3. Cut a big carrot into four pieces. You don't need to keep the second smallest piece.

4. Press the thickest piece of carrot into the brown paint. Press it onto paper to print a robin's body.

5. Press the piece of carrot into the paint again and print another body. Do this a few times.

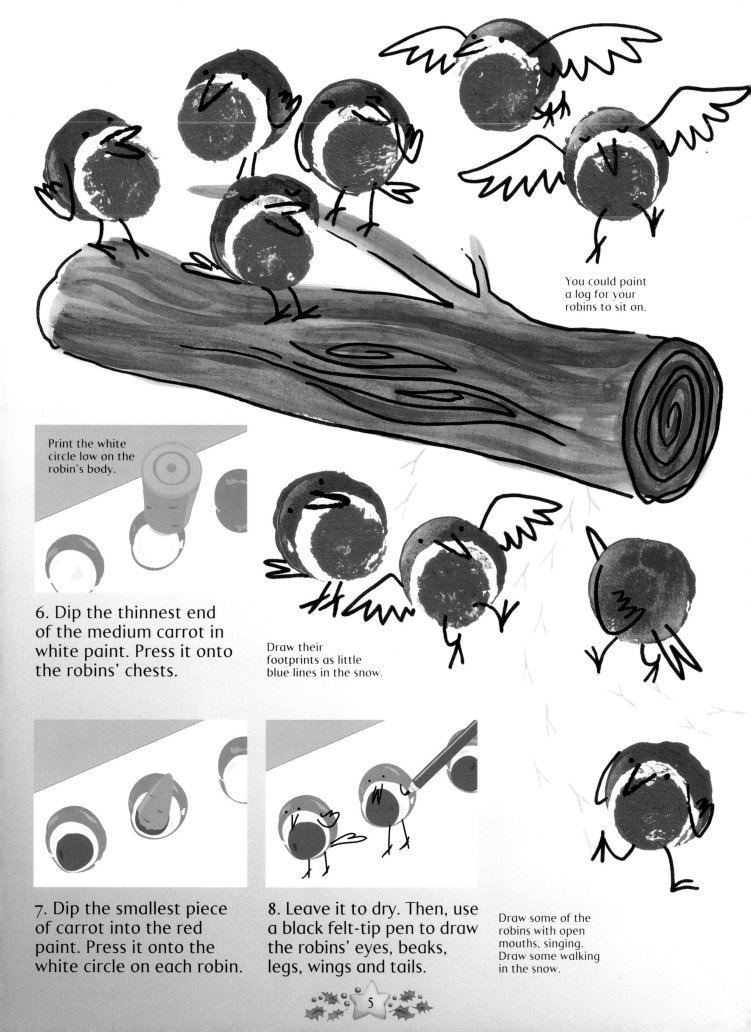

You could paint a log for your robins to sit on.

Print the white circle low on the robin's body.

6. Dip the thinnest end of the medium carrot in white paint. Press it onto the robins' chests.

Draw their footprints as little blue lines in the snow.

7. Dip the smallest piece of carrot into the red paint. Press it onto the white circle on each robin.

8. Leave it to dry. Then, use a black felt-tip pen to draw the robins' eyes, beaks, legs, wings and tails.

Draw some of the robins with open mouths, singing. Draw some walking in the snow.

Dancing angel chains

1. Fold a rectangle of white paper in half, so the two shorter edges meet. Then, fold it in half again.

2. Draw a circle, so that it almost touches the top of the paper. Draw a smaller circle inside it.

Make the small circle touch the bottom of the big one.

3. Draw a big triangle for a dress. Add little feet poking out from the bottom of the dress.

Make sure the hands touch the edges of the paper.

4. Draw two big sleeves almost reaching the edges of the paper. Add hands that go up to the edge.

5. Using a pair of scissors, cut around the angel, but don't cut along the folds around the hands.

6. Open out your chain of angels. Draw their faces and hair. Make each one look different.

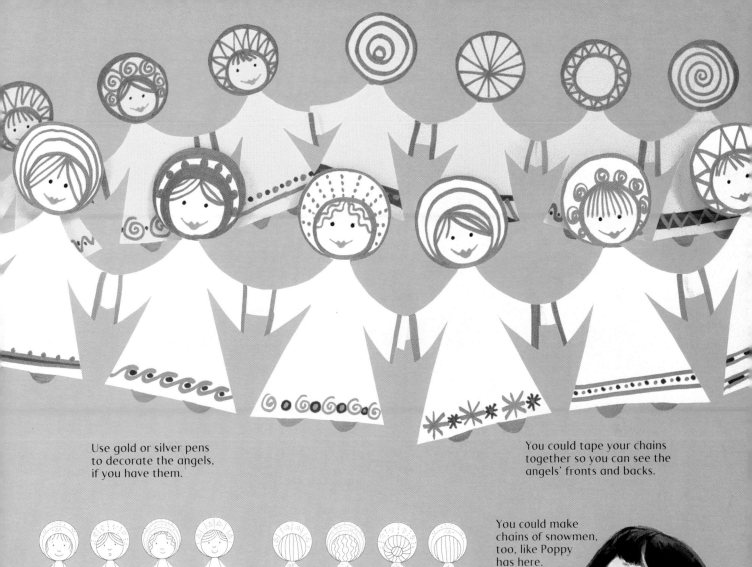

Use gold or silver pens to decorate the angels, if you have them.

You could tape your chains together so you can see the angels' fronts and backs.

7. Draw patterns on their dresses and on their halos. You could glue glitter on them, too.

8. Decorate the other side of the chain, too. Draw the backs of the angels. Add their hair and little wings.

You could make chains of snowmen, too, like Poppy has here.

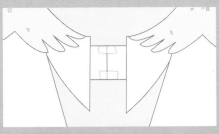

9. Make a few chains. Join them together by folding a little piece of tape around the angels' hands.

Dangly Santa and reindeer

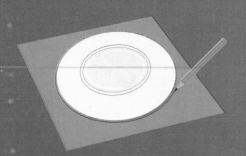

1. Put a big plate onto a piece of thick brown paper or thin cardboard. Draw around it in pencil.

2. Cut out the circle. Fold it in half, then open it out again. Cut along the fold to make two semicircles.

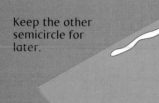

Keep the other semicircle for later.

3. Spread some glue about halfway along the flat edge of one of the semicircles, like this.

Hold the edges in place until they stick.

4. Hold the straight edge and bend the semicircle around to make a cone. Press the edges together.

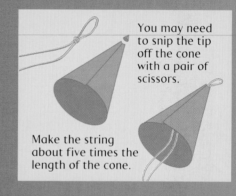

You may need to snip the tip off the cone with a pair of scissors.

Make the string about five times the length of the cone.

5. Cut a long piece of string. Fold it in half. Tie a knot in it to make a loop. Push the loop up through the cone.

6. Draw a reindeer head on the left-over semicircle of paper. Add wavy antlers, ears and a face.

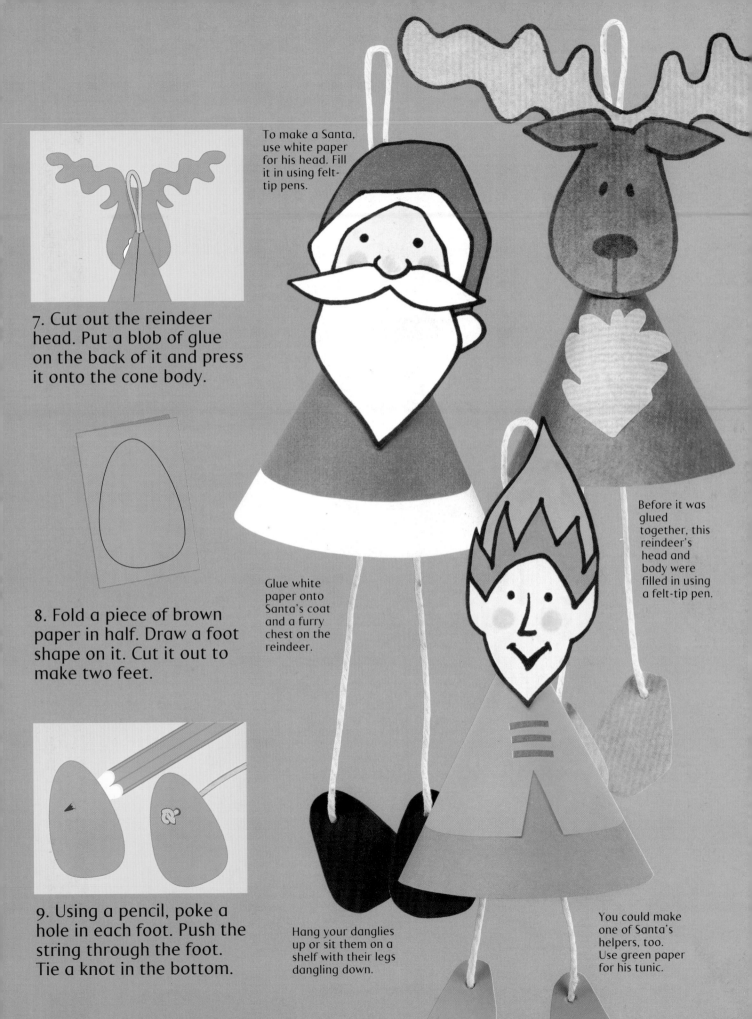

7. Cut out the reindeer head. Put a blob of glue on the back of it and press it onto the cone body.

8. Fold a piece of brown paper in half. Draw a foot shape on it. Cut it out to make two feet.

9. Using a pencil, poke a hole in each foot. Push the string through the foot. Tie a knot in the bottom.

To make a Santa, use white paper for his head. Fill it in using felt-tip pens.

Before it was glued together, this reindeer's head and body were filled in using a felt-tip pen.

Glue white paper onto Santa's coat and a furry chest on the reindeer.

Hang your danglies up or sit them on a shelf with their legs dangling down.

You could make one of Santa's helpers, too. Use green paper for his tunic.

Poppy's fir tree card

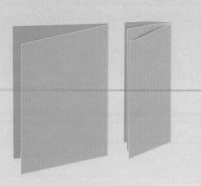

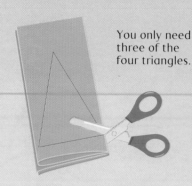

You only need three of the four triangles.

You can throw these parts away.

1. Fold a rectangle of green paper in half, so the two shorter edges meet. Then, fold it in half again.

2. Draw a long triangle on the folded paper. Cut it out, so you have four triangles the same size.

3. Cut a strip off one of the triangles and a bigger strip off another, like this, to make them different sizes.

Be careful not to cut any pieces all the way off.

4. Holding each triangle by its point, make lots of little snips along the bottom, to make a fringed edge.

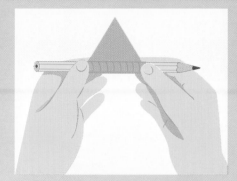

5. Curl the fringed end of each triangle around a pencil. This will make the fringe curly.

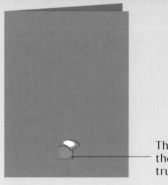

This is the tree trunk.

6. Fold a piece of thick blue paper in half. Cut out a little rectangle of brown paper. Glue it on, like this.

Match up the tops of the triangles.

7. Glue the biggest triangle onto the trunk. Glue the medium one on top, then the small one on top of that.

8. Dip your fingertip in white paint. Dab blobs on your tree and around it to make snowflakes.

9. Finger paint some snow on the ground. Add a star from the sticker page to the top of your tree.

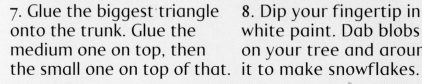

Stars and icicles

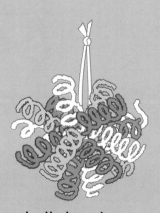

Star

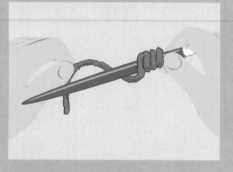

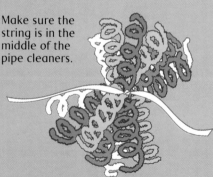

1. Hold one end of a pipe cleaner against the handle of a thin paintbrush. Wind the rest of the pipe cleaner tightly around the handle.

2. When the whole pipe cleaner is wound onto the handle, slide it off. Hold both ends and pull gently to make it a little longer.

3. Wind more pipe cleaners around the paintbrush in the same way, until you have ten curly pipe cleaners.

Make sure the string is in the middle of the pipe cleaners.

4. Lay a piece of thin string on a table. Put the pipe cleaners on top. Tie a tight knot in the middle of the pipe cleaners.

5. Bend all the pipe cleaners away from each other. Tie a knot in the top of the string. Then, hang up your curly star.

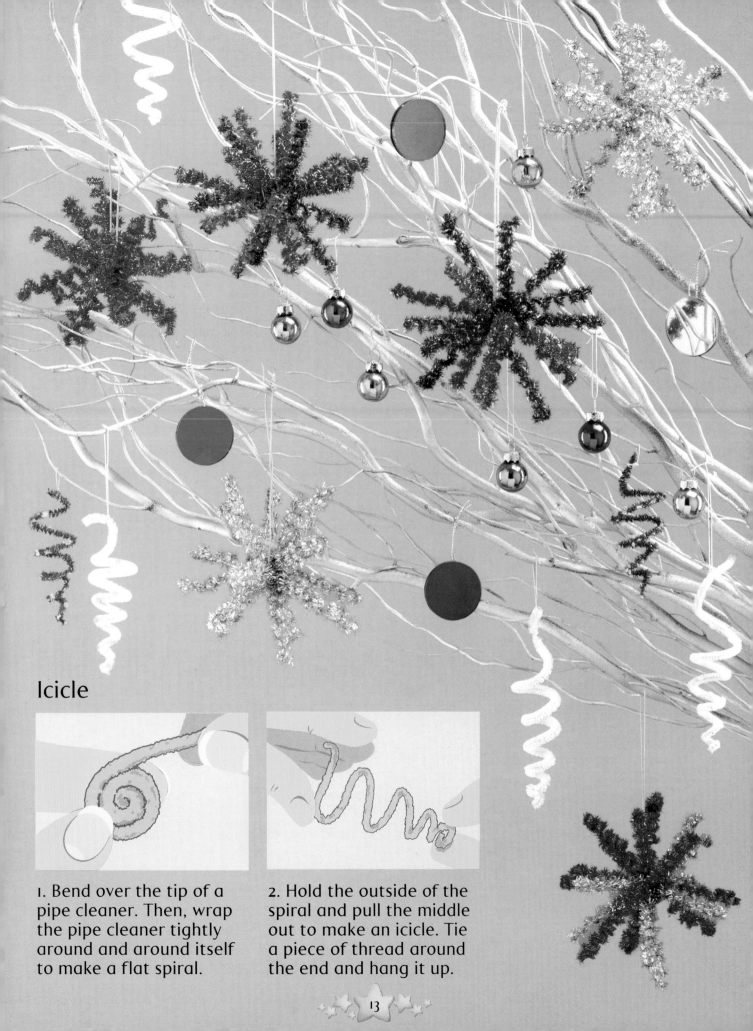

Icicle

1. Bend over the tip of a pipe cleaner. Then, wrap the pipe cleaner tightly around and around itself to make a flat spiral.

2. Hold the outside of the spiral and pull the middle out to make an icicle. Tie a piece of thread around the end and hang it up.

Mrs. Boot's mini Christmas trees

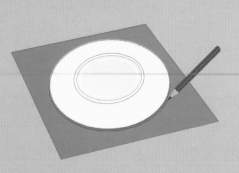

1. Put a small plate on top of a piece of thick green paper. Draw around it to make a circle.

Keep one of the semicircles to make another tree.

2. Cut out the circle. Fold it in half and then open it out. Cut along the fold to make two semicircles.

3. Spread some glue up to about halfway along the straight edge of one of the semicircles, like this.

Hold the edges in place until they stick.

4. Holding the straight edge, bend the semicircle around to make a cone. Press the edges together.

5. Put a mug on another piece of green paper. Draw around it to make a circle and cut it out.

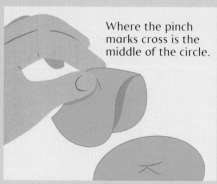

Where the pinch marks cross is the middle of the circle.

6. Bend the circle in half and pinch it in the middle. Bend it in half the other way and pinch it again.

Use white paper spirals to make snowy trees.

Sit these trees on a table or a window ledge as decorations.

You could use shiny paper to make the baubles.

7. Starting at the edge of the circle, draw a spiral line around and around until you reach the middle.

A blob of glue will hold the spiral in place.

8. Carefully cut along the line. Then, rest the spiral on the top of the cone tree so it hangs down.

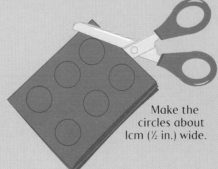

Make the circles about 1cm (½ in.) wide.

9. Fold a piece of red paper in half. Fold it in half again. Draw lots of circles and cut them out to make baubles.

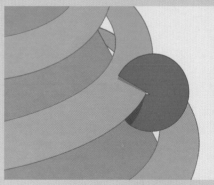

10. Cut into the middle of each circle. Slot them onto the edges of the spiral on the tree.

Festive bookmarks

1. On a piece of thin white cardboard, draw a teddy bear's head. Add a hat. Fill it all in with felt-tip pens.

2. Cut out the head. Put it on top of a piece of thin red cardboard. Draw around the head carefully.

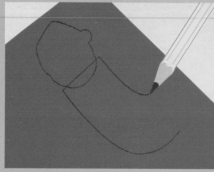

3. Draw a stocking shape, making sure that it overlaps the teddy bear's head a little at the top.

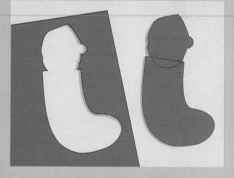

4. Carefully cut around the head and stocking shape. Don't cut under the teddy bear's chin.

You can hook the head over a page to mark your place in a book.

5. Spread glue on the top part of the head shape. Stick the bear's head on top. Make the hats line up.

Christmas writing paper

Dear Ted,
We are having a
Christmas party
tomorrow night.
We would love it
if you could come.
Best wishes, Mrs. B.

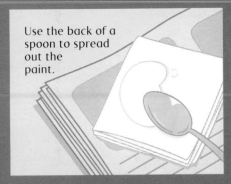

Use the back of a spoon to spread out the paint.

1. Spread out some old newspaper. Put a kitchen paper towel on it. Spread a little white paint on top.

Dear Ted,

Thank you for my great present.

Sam xXX

Dear Santa,

I would like a new bike with a basket.
Thank you.
Love,

Poppy x

Once the paper is dry, you could use it to write a letter to Santa or a thank-you letter.

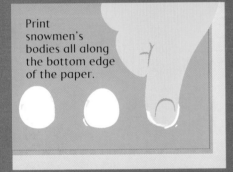

Print snowmen's bodies all along the bottom edge of the paper.

2. To print a snowman's body, press your thumb into the paint and press it onto a piece of blue paper.

3. Use the tip of your finger to print smaller blobs for heads on top of all the snowmen's bodies.

Add different kinds of hats and scarves.

4. Leave the paint to dry. Use felt-tip pens to draw their eyes, noses, mouths, buttons, hats and scarves.

Sam's Santa picture

Use the back of the spoon.

1. Put some kitchen paper towels on top of an old newspaper. Pour a little red paint onto them and spread it out with a spoon.

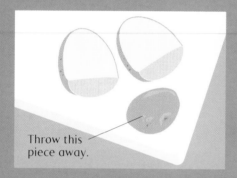

Throw this piece away.

2. Cut the end off a big potato and throw it away. Then, cut the rest of the potato in half. Keep one of the halves for later.

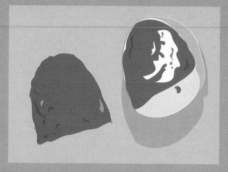

3. Dip one half of the potato into the red paint. Press it onto the middle of a piece of paper to print Santa's body.

4. Mix a little red and white paint together on an old saucer. Use a spoon to spread the pink paint onto a paper towel.

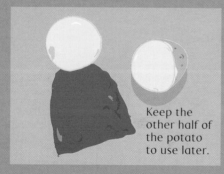

Keep the other half of the potato to use later.

5. Cut a small potato in half. Dip one half in the pink paint and press it onto the paper to print Santa's face.

6. Dip your finger in the red paint and finger paint an arm. Dip it in again to paint the other arm. Then, finger paint his legs.

7. Dip your finger in red paint and finger paint Santa's hat. Dip your finger in again and paint his mittens. Let the paint dry.

You could finger print snowflakes on your picture and paint some snow on the ground.

Use the left-over halves of the potatoes to print a snowman.

8. Dip your finger in some white paint. Press it on Santa's chin. Keep dipping your finger and printing blobs to make his beard.

9. Do finger prints around the edges of his hat, body, arms and legs. Finger print a bobble on his hat. Leave it to dry.

10. Using a black felt-tip pen, draw two dots for Santa's eyes. Add his nose and a smiling mouth. Draw his boots and fill them in.

Mrs. Boot's glittery paper chains

You could use glitter glue instead, if you have it.

1. Dab blobs of glue all over a piece of paper about the size of this page. Sprinkle glitter on top.

Use the left-over glitter to decorate another piece of paper.

2. When the glue is dry, tip the extra glitter onto an old newspaper. Decorate some more paper.

3. When all the glue is dry, cut across the pieces of paper to make lots of short strips.

Make sure the glitter is on the outside.

4. Bend one of the strips into a loop and tape it into place. Thread another loop through and tape it.

5. Keep on threading and taping loops until you have made a long chain. Hang the chain up.

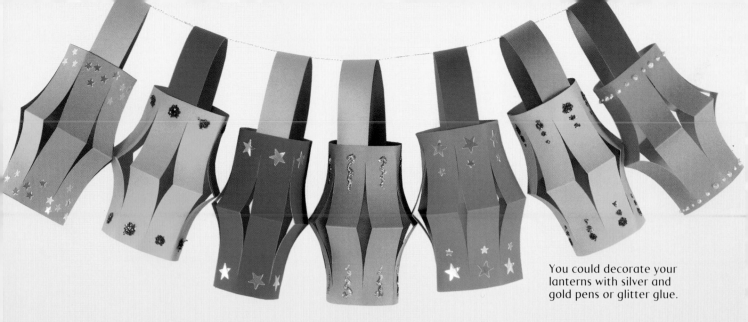

You could decorate your lanterns with silver and gold pens or glitter glue.

Paper lanterns

Save half of the paper to make another lantern later.

Don't cut all the way up to the top.

This strip will be a handle for the lantern.

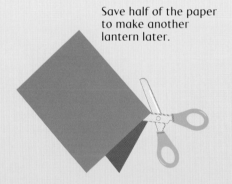

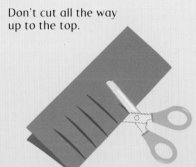

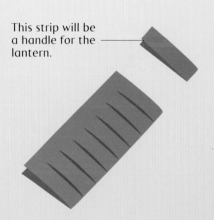

1. Fold a piece of thick paper about the size of this page in half. Cut down the fold to make two pieces.

2. Fold one of the pieces of paper in half so that the long sides meet. Make cuts all along the folded side.

3. Cut the last strip all the way off the folded piece of paper. Keep this strip to use later.

Decorate your paper lanterns with stickers from the sticker page.

4. Open the piece of paper out. Spread glue along one of the short edges. Press it onto the other short edge.

5. Put glue on both ends of the strip of paper you cut off in step 3. Press it onto the top of the lantern.

Poppy's pom-pom snowballs

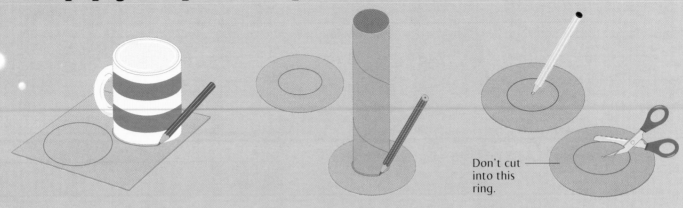

1. Put a mug on top of a piece of cardboard and draw around it twice. Cut out the two circles using a pair of scissors.

2. Draw around a cardboard tube or a small jar lid to make a smaller circle inside each of your cut-out circles.

3. Using a ballpoint pen, poke a hole through the middle of each cardboard circle. Then, cut out the circles inside them.

Don't cut into this ring.

Use white sparkly wool or yarn if you have it.

Make sure the wool will fit through the cardboard rings.

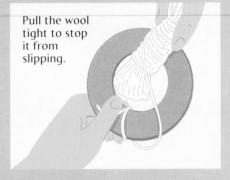

Pull the wool tight to stop it from slipping.

4. Hold the end of a ball of wool, or yarn, with your thumb and wind it around your hand. Keep winding until the wool is quite thick.

5. Pull the loops of wool off your hand. Hold one end and wind the rest of the wool around the middle of the loops.

6. Put the two cardboard rings together. Hold the end of the wool with your thumb. Wind the rest over and through the ring.

7. Keep winding the wool around the rings. Turn the ring as you wind so the wool is even. Keep going until you run out of wool.

8. Poke scissors between the two rings, like this. Cut all around the rings to separate the wool into strands.

Hang the pom-pom snowballs on your Christmas tree.

Ask for some help to tie this in a very tight knot.

9. Pull the two rings apart a little. Tie a long piece of string tight around the middle between the two rings. Tie a double knot.

You can trim any long pieces off the pom-pom.

10. Tie a knot in the top of the string so you can hang the pom-pom up. Cut the rings of cardboard and pull them out.

Sam and Rusty's striped stars

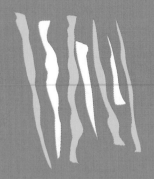

Make the strips overlap one other.

When you cut them out you will have six circles.

1. Rip some orange and white tissue paper into lots of thin strips. They don't need to be the same width.

2. Lay a piece of yellow tissue paper onto a piece of plastic food wrap. Glue the tissue strips onto it.

3. Fold a piece of paper the size of this page in half. Draw around a mug three times. Cut the circles out.

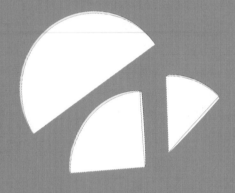

You can throw this piece away.

Cut a fairly deep 'v', like this.

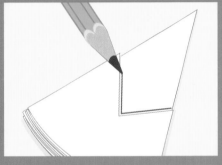

4. Fold one of the circles in half. Fold it in half again and then once more, to make a pointed shape.

5. Fold the other circles in the same way. Cut a 'v' shape into the tip of one of the folded circles.

6. Place the cut circle on top of another folded circle. Draw around the 'v' shape and cut it out.

The cut-out shape makes a star.

7. Draw the same 'v' shape on the other folded circles and cut them out. Open all of the circles.

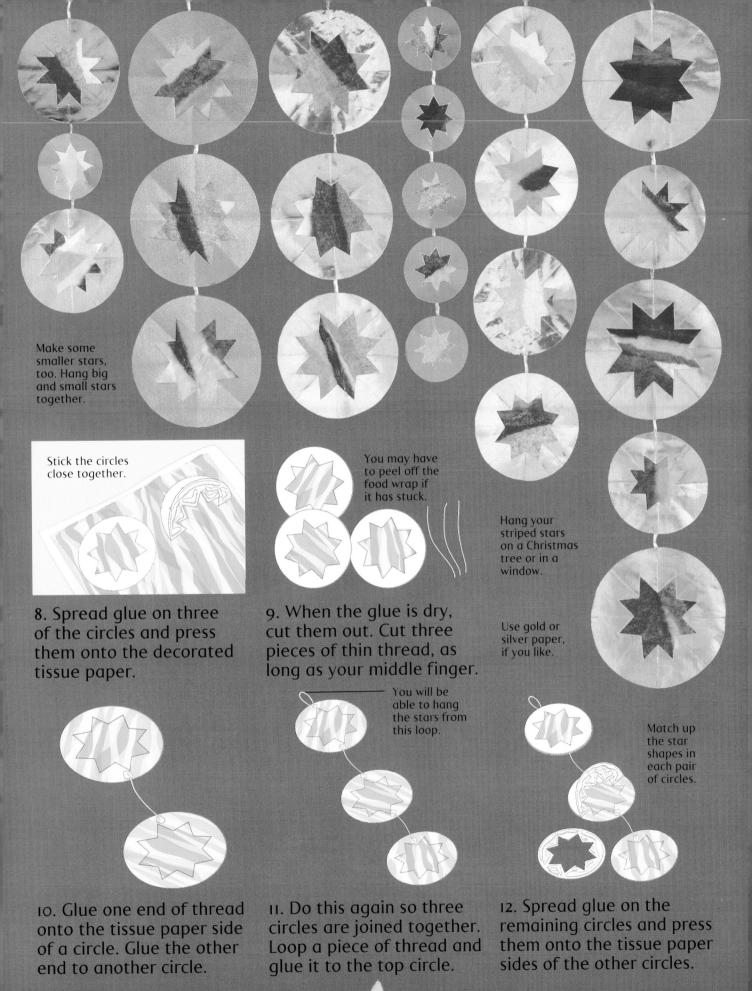

Make some smaller stars, too. Hang big and small stars together.

Stick the circles close together.

8. Spread glue on three of the circles and press them onto the decorated tissue paper.

You may have to peel off the food wrap if it has stuck.

9. When the glue is dry, cut them out. Cut three pieces of thin thread, as long as your middle finger.

You will be able to hang the stars from this loop.

Hang your striped stars on a Christmas tree or in a window.

Use gold or silver paper, if you like.

Match up the star shapes in each pair of circles.

10. Glue one end of thread onto the tissue paper side of a circle. Glue the other end to another circle.

11. Do this again so three circles are joined together. Loop a piece of thread and glue it to the top circle.

12. Spread glue on the remaining circles and press them onto the tissue paper sides of the other circles.

Pop-up Santa card

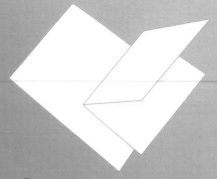
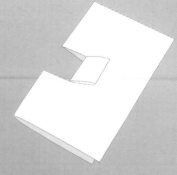

1. Cut out two rectangles of paper the same size. Fold one of them in half, so the short edges meet.

You could write a big Christmas greeting on the outside of the card and sign your name on the inside.

2. Make two cuts in the folded edge of the paper. Fold the flap between the cuts over, like this.

You could stick stars in the sky from the sticker pages.

3. Fold the flap onto the other side of the card, too, and crease it. Then, unfold the flap and open the card.

4. Pinch along the middle fold on either side of the flap. Don't do this on the flap, only along the fold.

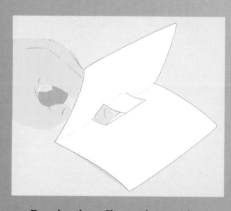

5. Push the flap down into the card, like this. Then carefully close the card and smooth it out flat.

Don't get any glue on the flap.

6. Open the card. The flap will pop up like a box. Fold the other rectangle in half. Glue it onto the back.

7. Cut a piece of white paper to fit in the card, like this. Use a pencil to mark the edges of the flap on it.

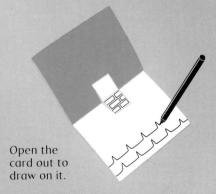

Open the card out to draw on it.

8. Draw a Santa up to his waist. Make his body fit between the pencil marks. Fill him in with felt-tip pens.

9. Draw bricks on the flap. Add roof tiles to the bottom half of the card. Fill the rest in with blue.

10. Cut out your Santa. Put a blob of glue near the top of the chimney. Then, stick Santa onto the chimney.

Apple Tree Farm angel

Keep one semicircle for later.

1. Put a big plate on top of some thick white paper. Using a pencil, draw around the plate to make a circle. Cut it out.

2. Fold the circle in half. Cut along the fold to make two semicircles. One will be the angel's dress. Decorate it using felt-tip pens.

Stand your angel on a table or put her on the top of your Christmas tree.

3. Let your decorations dry. Then, glue about halfway along the straight edge of the semicircle, like this.

You could use gold pens and glitter glue to decorate your angel.

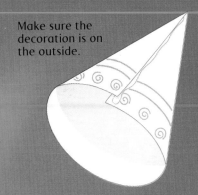

Make sure the decoration is on the outside.

4. Bend the semicircle around and press the straight edges together to make a cone. Hold it in place until it sticks.

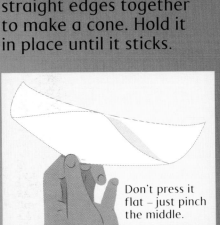

Don't press it flat – just pinch the middle.

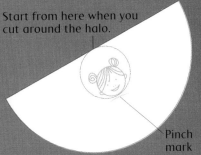

Start from here when you cut around the halo.

Pinch mark

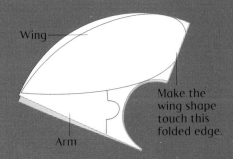

Wing

Make the wing shape touch this folded edge.

Arm

5. Bend the other semicircle in half so the curved edge touches the straight edge. Pinch the middle a little. Open it out again.

6. Draw a head, making the chin touch the pinch mark. Add a circle for a halo, reaching the edge of the paper. Cut around the halo.

7. Fold the rest of the semicircle in half. Draw a wing shape on it like this. Draw an arm shape in the space left below the wing.

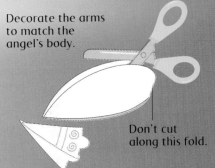

Decorate the arms to match the angel's body.

Don't cut along this fold.

Turn them around as you dip them in, to get glitter all around the edge.

Hold the head, wings and arms in place until they stick.

8. Cut the arm shape out to make two arms. Then, cut out the wing shape. Don't cut along the folded side of the wings.

9. Pour glitter into an old saucer. Spread glue along the edges of the halo and the wings. Dip them in the glitter. Let them dry.

10. Put a blob of glue on the head. Press it onto the body. Spread glue on the arms and the middle of the wings. Press them on, too.

Snowflake giftwrap

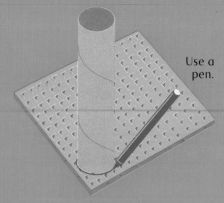

Use a pen.

1. On a piece of sponge cloth, draw around a cardboard tube to make a circle. If you don't have a tube, use a small jar lid.

When you have finished it will look like a snowflake, like this.

Spread the glue on the side you drew on.

2. Inside the circle, draw an 'x' shape, and then draw a '+' shape on top, like this, to make a snowflake shape.

3. Cut out the circle. Then, cut out little triangles in between each of the lines you have drawn. Don't cut all the way to the middle.

4. On a piece of cardboard, draw around the cardboard tube to make a circle. Cut it out. Spread glue on the snowflake and press it on.

If you don't have a cork, then use a plastic bottle top.

Use the back of the spoon to spread the paint.

Let this paper dry before you use it to wrap gifts.

5. Spread glue on the end of a cork. Press it into the middle of the cardboard circle. This is a stamp you can use to print with.

6. Put some kitchen paper towels on top of an old newspaper. Pour a little white paint on top. Spread it out with a spoon.

7. Dip the stamp into the paint and press it onto a big piece of blue paper to print a snowflake. Keep on doing this until the paper is full.

You could print gift tags to match your giftwrap.

Try printing snowflakes on strips of gold paper and sticking them onto plain paper.

Write inside your
tag and tape it to
a wrapped-up gift.

Glue your shiny
shapes onto
cardboard
circles or
stars.

Shiny gift tags

Make sure the
shiniest side is
on the outside.

Press firmly
as you
draw.

1. Fold a small rectangle
of kitchen foil in half.
Spread glue on the inside
and press it together.

2. Resting on a pile of
old newspapers, use a
ballpoint pen or a pencil
to draw a triangle.

3. Turn the foil around.
Then, draw another
triangle on top, to
make a star.

Spread the
glue on the
side you
drew on.

4. Add some dots and tiny
stars. Turn the foil over
and glue it onto a small
folded piece of cardboard.

Series editor: Fiona Watt • Art Director: Mary Cartwright • Photographic manipulation: Emma Julings
First published in 2003 by Usborne Publishing Ltd., Usborne House, 83-85 Saffron Hill, London, England. www.usborne.com Copyright © 2003 Usborne Publishing Ltd.